GREEN ZONE

Living

2nd Edition

- 7 Steps to a
HAPPY, HEALTHY and
PEACEFUL LIFESTYLE

DR. K. SOHAIL MBBS FRCP(C)
&
BETTE DAVIS RN BN MN

GREEN ZONE

Living

2nd Edition

- 7 Steps to a

HAPPY, HEALTHY and

PEACEFUL LIFESTYLE

DR. K. SOHAIL MBBS FRCP(C)

&

BETTE DAVIS RN BN MN

GREENZONE Publishing

2013, Whitby, Ontario, Canada

First Edition 2008
Second Edition 2013

Copyright ©2013 by Dr. K. Sohail and Bette
Davis RN BN MN

Published in 2008, 2013 by GREENZONE Publishing, a
division of Dr. Sohail MPC Ltd.
213 Byron Street South
Whitby, Ontario, Canada L1N4P7
T. 905-666-7253 F, 905-666-4397
Website: greenzoneliving.ca

**National Library of Canada Cataloguing in
Publication**
Sohail, K. (Khalid), 1952-
Davis B. (Bette), 1952-
Green Zone Living – 7 Steps to a Happy, Healthy &Peaceful
Lifestyle / K. Sohail, B Davis

ISBN 978-0-9810038-0-1
1. Interpersonal relations. 2. Psychology,
I. Title.

Editing Cover and Text Design	Bette Davis
Cover Design	Shahid Shafiq Nusoft Technologies

DEDICATED TO…

the dream of
creating a peaceful world together.

ACKNOWLEDGEMENTS

Our heartfelt gratitude to our many clients and colleagues for their inspiration and willingness to share their stories and experiences so that others could benefit.

We owe a very special thanks to Deana Seymore who handles the numerous document changes with grace and a smile.

We are also very grateful to Michael Thompson who orchestrates the book printing process. His conscientiousness and reliability is incredibly reassuring.

Shahid Shafiq and Furqan Khan of *Nusoft Technologies* deserve a special debt of gratitude for their determination, creativity and foresight in bringing our message to the wider audience.

And last but certainly not least, to our Dear ones, those whom we call our *Family of the Heart*, we wish to extend our love and thankfulness for all of the ways in which they care for us and support our dreams.

Sohail and Bette

CONTENTS

FOREWORD

It is always a privilege to be a part of another project on mental health, particularly the Green Zone and especially with Sohail, my co-traveler on life's journeys. Many who read our books and attended our seminars, have asked about our creative relationship. We have known each other for 35 years having been introduced in 1978 at the Waterford Hospital in St. John's, Newfoundland. As young professionals, Sohail was a Resident in Psychiatry and I was a beginning Mental Health Nurse, we were both eager to be therapists and to fulfill our dream of being part of a clinic, like Creative Psychotherapy Clinic. Since then, both of us have travelled different paths but came back together as colleagues, co-therapists, co-authors and life partners.

In our clinic we not only teach the Green Zone concept to our clients but live it as a core value of our personal and professional philosophy. At work we structure our therapies, meetings and schedule so that we and our staff are more likely to stay in the Green

Zone. At home, Green Zone principles guide how we live, grow and resolve conflicts with our family.

In addition, people have also asked us how we work together as co-authors. Many co-authors have a rhythm that works for them. Ours is a rather unique collaboration that reflects our individual strengths and the strengths of our relationship. We usually begin with the goal of talking about and collaborating on the entire book, so that each of us feels that we are a part of the whole book no matter who writes a particular chapter. For simplicity, those written from my point of view are identified as such while those written from both perspectives and Sohail's are unmarked.

As always, it is our sincere wish that each book we write helps ever-increasing numbers of people to live their lives with purpose, joy and contentment.

Yours in the Green,
Bette

Dr. K. Sohail & Bette Davis

Introduction

GIVING BIRTH TO THE
GREEN ZONE PHILOSOPHY

Dear Reader,

I feel very excited to share my Green Zone Philosophy with you, as it has been very special and precious to me. It inspires me and helps me create and grow every day. I hope it becomes as meaningful to you as it has been to me.

You may have never heard of this Green Zone Philosophy that I am going to share with you. You might be wondering, where did it come from? For the last few years I have been giving birth to this philosophy and lifestyle. For me giving birth is a wonderful metaphor as it is a creative metaphor.

Green Zone Living

When I started my Creative Psychotherapy Clinic in 1995, in Whitby Ontario, Canada, I asked my dear colleague, Anne Henderson to join me as I had a lot of respect for her and she had inspired me over the years. Anne bought everything for the clinic. The only thing I bought was a statue, a statue of a woman giving birth to a baby, giving birth to herself. That has been my metaphor of therapy, of creativity and of life.

We are all giving birth to ourselves, without being aware of it. I believe human sufferings are our labour pains. Being born from our mother's womb is our physical birth but to discover our real worth, our real talent, our real potential and our special gift is our creative birth. Some of us are more successful than others. One philosopher said, 'Most of us die before we are fully born'.

Dr. K. Sohail & Bette Davis

So I was talking about giving birth to the Green Zone Philosophy. It happened a few years ago when I was fifty. Most people reach creative menopause by that age but I was lucky to finally deliver after a prolonged pregnancy and strong labour pains. It was painful and exciting at the same time. It was a wonderful experience. I had to wait a long time but it was worth waiting for.

Around that time my dear friend, Bette Davis, moved from Newfoundland to Ontario to continue writing the Green Zone Books with me and she asked me, "How do you feel about giving birth to the Green Zone Philosophy?" I told her that it was one of the most exciting encounters of my entire life. When she asked me how it changed my life I shared with her that it:

♦ helped me find peace within myself and harmony with others

♦ assisted me in creating a healthy and happy lifestyle, and

♦ enabled me to serve other human beings in my professional and social lives.

Over the years I had:

♦ pursued different hobbies, passions and dreams,

♦ traveled to different parts of the world,

♦ studied different schools of thought,

♦ read hundreds of books,

♦ interviewed dozens of writers, artists and philosophers, and

♦ treated thousands of patients.

Gradually my observations, experiences and introspections came together. From conception to creation was a slow, prolonged delivery and labour but giving birth to the Green Zone Philosophy, writing a series of books and offering seminars was a wonderful experience.

It was like:

♦ the colours of the rainbow transforming into white light,

Dr. K. Sohail & Bette Davis

♦ discovering a refined silk thread that helped me connect all those beads of knowledge and experience together that I had been collecting throughout my life, and

♦ creating a new paradigm of a happy, healthy and peaceful lifestyle for myself and others.

In my eyes the Green Zone Philosophy is a philosophy that:

♦ helps people have a better understanding of themselves and

♦ encourages them to discover unique gifts in their personalities and lives, develop them and then share them with others.

I feel fortunate that I have not only conceived and delivered the Green Zone Philosophy, I am also able to practice it myself everyday in my personal life and teach it in my professional life as a psychotherapist.

I find teaching and learning very exciting as they broaden my existential horizons. I like to

Green Zone Living

teach what I practice and practice what I teach. The Green Zone Philosophy is a journey from a Green Zone Day to a Green Zone Week to a Green Zone Lifestyle. This journey in our personal and social lives extends from childhood to old age. Giving birth to the Green Zone Philosophy and practicing it has helped me grow as a person, therapist and a writer and I hope that I keep on growing until the day I die. Now I live in my Green Zone and help others to discover and then live in their Green Zone.

When my first Green Zone Book was ready to go to the printer my valued friend and publisher, Bill Belfontaine and I had a serious discussion about the book title. Initially it was titled *The Art of Living in the Green Zone* and after a lengthy discussion we agreed to change the name to *The Art of Living in Your Green Zone* as we believe that each human being has his/her

Dr. K. Sohail & Bette Davis

own unique Green Zone which some of us have yet to discover.

After writing a series of Green Zone Books I might have stopped writing but my dear friend, Aamir Hasan inspired me to write another book. He believed that my previous books focused more on my patients many of whom suffered from serious emotional problems. Their stories in those books highlighted their struggles to travel from their painful Yellow and distressing Red Zones to their healthy Green Zones. Aamir believed that my Green Zone Philosophy was not restricted to people with emotional problems and could assist all human beings from diverse social, professional and cultural backgrounds to improve their quality of life. So he encouraged me to write another book that would address all people whether they have an emotional problem or not. So the credit for this book goes to Aamir Hasan who is a creative artist and has believed in the Green Zone Philosophy from the very beginning. He inspired me to create a new Green Zone Living website www.greenzoneliving.ca and put more emphasis on helping others through our seminars.

The final question is whether this book has any value for you. Will it inspire you to change your life or will you find it a waste of time? It is hard for me to predict whether you have a closed mind or you are open to new ideas and believe in life long learning.

At this stage I am reminded of a folktale of an old Indian Darvesh who left his village and went to the jungle to find nirvana. After twenty years of fasting, traveling and meditating, he found enlightenment and got in touch with his truth. He wanted to go back to his village and serve his community and share his truth with them. On his way back he had to cross a river. When he arrived at the shore of the river he met a boatman. Darvesh asked the boatman if he would take him to the other side of the river so that he could go to his village. The boatman looked at his tattered attire and said, "It will cost you ten pesos"

"I do not have any money but I will pray for you."

"I do not need your prayers, I need your ten pesos to feed my family."

After listening to that, Darvesh walked away peacefully. A couple of hours later when the boat was full of passengers, the boatman crossed the river. When he reached the other side he saw the Darvesh already there.

"How did you get here?" boatman asked in bewilderment.

"By meditating for twenty years, I have learnt the art of walking on water." Darvesh said in an affectionate way.

Green Zone Living

The young boatman, who was a cynical man laughed and said, "Your twenty years of meditation is only worth ten pesos."

So I am sharing with you what I have learnt in my twenty years of personal and professional experiences. After reading the book, if you say it is only worth ten pesos, I will not be offended. I know my Green Zone Philosophy has helped not only me become a better writer, a better therapist, a better friend and most of all a better human being but it has also helped many of my friends, colleagues and patients grow. I hope you discover your special gift, your Green Zone, your dream and your meaning in life.

Wishing you all the best,
Sohail

Dr. K. Sohail & Bette Davis

Chapter One

7 STEP SELF-HELP PROGRAM – FROM A GREEN ZONE DAY TO A GREEN ZONE LIFESTYLE

FIRST STEP - AWARENESS OF YOUR EMOTIONAL ZONES

Whether you are a teacher or a nurse, a home-maker or the president of a company, a lawyer or a professor, a farmer or a businessman, you are always able to improve the quality of your life

Green Zone Living

and create a happy, healthy and peaceful lifestyle that I call Green Zone Living. But before I share with you the details of that philosophy and practice, you need to know that the Green Zone Philosophy is based on the concept of three imaginary Emotional Zones. I call them the Green, Yellow and Red Zones, using the image of the traffic lights. When you are relaxed and happy and enjoying life you are in your Green Zone. When you are mildly frustrated and irritated, or sad and anxious, you are in your Yellow Zone and when you lose control and get angry or get depressed and distressed and completely withdraw, you are in your Red Zone. Individuals are unique and experience their Emotional Zones in their own unique way. This book is an attempt to help you get in touch with your Green Zone and then live there.

Dr. K. Sohail & Bette Davis

The first step towards creating a Green Zone Lifestyle is to become aware of what Emotional Zone you are in at any particular time. It is a simple but a profound step. Awareness is the most significant factor to helping you stay in your Green Zone. By becoming aware of your Emotional Zones you gain control. Awareness of how you are feeling emotionally at any moment is incredibly empowering. To make any conscious change in your life, you need to feel in control, strong and powerful. It is amazing how this simple awareness can give you more control and power.

The fact of life is that most of us live our day to day lives without really acknowledging appreciating or cherishing the moment. We do not live in the moment.

We think without really thinking.

We feel without really feeling.

Green Zone Living

We talk and act without really being aware of the effects of our words and actions on others or even on ourselves.

When you are aware, you are better able to make emotionally intelligent decisions about how you will deal with your day-to-day dilemmas in a rational, constructive and mature way. If you are not aware, then you can easily be distracted and pushed into the distressing Yellow Zone or pulled into the painful Red Zone.

SECOND STEP - RECOGNIZING CHANGES IN YOUR EMOTIONAL ZONES

As you become aware of your Emotional Zones, you then begin to notice the changes in your day-to-day life. Such awareness will help you in recognizing the patterns of your emotions.

I have suggested to many people to keep a daily record of their Emotional Zones in their Green Zone Diary. At the back of this book, you will find sample page - *Discovering Your Green Day* - which you can use as a guide to structure your Green Zone Diary. At the end of each day, take a couple of minutes to reflect on your day and complete a page in your Green Zone Diary, highlighting how many hours you spent in each Zone and what was happening at that time. By spending a few minutes every day for a couple of weeks, you will be able to identify:

Green Zone Living

- all those people and situations that are associated with your Green Zone, as well as
- all those upsetting people and stressful situations that are related to your Yellow and Red Zones.

Next you need to reflect on those people and situations, as they are a key to recognizing many of your positive and negative patterns. They will help you to spot and change your emotional patterns.

In addition to looking at your emotional patterns linked to external factors, you need to also consider the internal factors, such as your inner dialogue, the comments - either negative or positive, accurate or inaccurate – that we all make on an ongoing basis through out our day. This inner commentary plays a major role in our self-esteem, how we perceive and interpret external factors and stimuli. It has been my observation and experience as a psychotherapist that people with low self-confidence and poor self-esteem develop a negative thought pattern and become their own worst enemies. People frequently say to themselves:

- I am not good enough
- I am a loser
- I am a failure as a parent, worker, even as a human being.

If you have any of those negative patterns, they can easily keep you in your Yellow and Red Zones and as well lead you to interpret life experiences in a negative way putting meanings onto life encounters that others do not see. Because of your poor self-esteem and negative self-image you can put negative meanings in your life experiences and find reasons, justifications even rationalizations to stay in your Yellow and Red Zones. I share with such people that Green Zone people *act* while Red Zone people *react*.

Green Zone Living

A wise man once said that life is an ocean and the human heart is like a boat. As long as the boat is intact one does not have to worry about the outside water but if there is a hole in the boat and two gallons of water come inside the boat, those two gallons of water are more dangerous than the two million gallons of water in the ocean. People with positive self-esteem have a heart that is intact but people with negative self-esteem have a heart with a hole and the stresses of life can easily come in and cause distress or depression.

Dr. K. Sohail & Bette Davis

THIRD STEP - RECOVERING FROM YOUR YELLOW AND RED ZONES

After *recognizing* the negative patterns the next step is learning to *recover* from your Yellow and Red Zones. It is a step towards empowering yourself and taking control of your own life. When you let someone push you into the Yellow Zone or let a situation pull you into the Red Zone, it means that you were vulnerable and you gave your power to that person or situation. But after you fall into a Red Zone ditch, it is your responsibility to *recover* and come back to your Green Zone. We are all human and we are all pushed into the Yellow or Red Zone from time to time but it is better to drive through the Yellow and Red Zone rather than park there for a long time.

Recovering from the Yellow and Red Zone might be as simple as taking some time off and relaxing or getting some support from a friend or a consultation with a wise woman or man. Your dear ones can offer you the reassurance and support that you need but you may need to ask for it, as they cannot read your mind and heart. You have to call them or visit them or invite them and share your dilemma and ask their friendly advice. By doing so you will look after yourself and decrease your suffering.

Dr. K. Sohail & Bette Davis

FOURTH STEP - RESTRAINING FROM GOING TO THE YELLOW AND RED ZONES

After *recognizing* your positive and negative patterns and learning to *recover* from Yellow and Red Zones you are ready for the next step. It is the step of *restraining*. Now that you are aware that some people push you into the Yellow Zone and some situations pull you into the Red Zone, you can sit down and reflect upon all the ways in which you can handle these situations differently and *restrain* from entering the Yellow and Red Zones in the future. If you have reached a stage of helplessness in life you might think that there is no way out and you are trapped but in reality there are always different options and choices available to deal with a situation that you have never thought of before. If you discuss your situation with dear friends you will be surprised

Green Zone Living

how a different point of view can help you find new ways to deal with old problems.

After those discussions you can plan a strategy to deal with your Yellow Zone people and Red Zone situations. You might be able to avoid some of these situations and people completely or decrease the frequency or intensity of the interaction. So let's consider some of the techniques we use at our clinic to stay in the Green Zone.

CREATING AN EMOTIONAL RAINCOAT

Over the years I have developed the concept of the Emotional Raincoat. Many of my friends and clients find that concept very helpful in dealing with stressful situations. Let me give you a couple of examples.

1. On Friday afternoons after work if I am going to visit a friend, I realize that I have

to deal with the Red Zone traffic. To create my Emotional Raincoat I call my friend before leaving so that he does not worry if I am late for dinner. I also take my favourite music CD on which I have taped all my favourite singers from Kenny Rogers to Kenny G and I listen to them in the jammed traffic so that I do not get stressed by the hustle and bustle.

2. One of my clients loves his brother but does not like his sister-in-law. He believes his brother married a 'bitch' who turns into a 'witch' when she is angry. To cope with that situation he meets his brother in a restaurant or a park or on the beach and avoids his sister-in-law. That is his Emotional Raincoat.

3. One of my friends loves his sister but does not like his brother-in-law. She thinks her sister married a 'jerk' who

Green Zone Living

turns into a 'wolf' when he is angry. Her Emotional Raincoat is her nephews and nieces. When the children are around the brother-in-law is respectful.

4. One of our colleagues realized that his mother made a lot of critical Red Zone comments to him when he saw her on his own but not when they were with family. Instantaneously he was able to bring their relationship into the Green by asking his sister and her family, with whom he had a Green Zone relationship, to join them when they got together.

After you have created Emotional Raincoats for different stressful situations you will be surprised how your number of hours in the Green Zone will increase and your number of hours in the Red Zone will be reduced resulting in a major change in your life. Many friends, colleagues and clients have doubled their Green Zone Hours within a few weeks using these techniques.

CREATING A SPECIAL GREEN ZONE HOUR EACH DAY

To increase the Green Zone Hours in your life you can plan a special Green Zone Hour each day which can be devoted to doing all those things that you like to do, want to do and love to do. You can share with your family and friends that you have decided to take care of your mental health - to enjoy life and you are going to have a Green Zone Hour every day. You will be surprised that in most cases your relatives and friends will be very supportive.

Many people that I know who have been successful with this program started with:

- going for a walk

- reading a book
- going to the library
- visiting a park
- going to the beach
- listening to music
- playing with children or
- spending time with a dear friend.

By doing activities that are enjoyable, you are indirectly telling yourself and others that you are important and that it is valuable to spend time nurturing yourself. Your Green Zone Hour is important in learning to like yourself and enjoying your own company. Don't you think that it will be hard for others to like you and enjoy your company if you do not like yourself and enjoy your own company?

Your Green Zone Hours will gradually help you develop an interest that you enjoy. It might be worthwhile for you to pursue a hobby that can turn into a passion. You might like to follow a dream that you always wanted to pursue as a teenager but because of school, family and work responsibilities, you let it go. Maybe it is time to review your week and give yourself an evening each week for a hobby, a passion or a dream. This time will be your date with yourself or with your dear friends to have some fun. Whether you play tennis or racquet ball, work in your garden or paint, read poetry or join a team, all those activities will not only increase your happiness in life but also help you make a circle of close friends that I call my *Family of the Heart*. Such a family is your chosen and adopted family who accept you for who you are. If you do not have a nurturing and supportive biological family, then there is more need for you to have a Family of the Heart who can help you live in your Green Zone. If you would like to know more about how other people got in touch

Green Zone Living

with their Green Zone and started living in it, you might like to read our book, *The Art of Living in Your Green Zone*.

FIFTH STEP - CREATING GREEN ZONE RELATIONSHIPS

Like individuals, relationships also have a personality, character and lifestyle. As well, intimate relationships have a life cycle of their own. They are born, they grow and they die, either by separation, divorce or death. I encourage people to assess the quality of their relationships and discover the Zone in which each of them is living.

Healthy relationships thrive in the Green Zone and have Green Zone communication styles. In such relationships people feel free to spontaneously express their affection and are able to resolve their conflicts.

Unhealthy relationships live in the Yellow and Red Zones. In such relationships people feel inhibited and tense. Seldom is there a free flow of feelings and the differences turn into conflicts. In such relationships, resolving the problems becomes very difficult and in many cases people need a mediator or a therapist to assist them to find their way.

THREE WAYS TO DEAL WITH CONFLICTS – RESOLVING, DISSOLVING, MEDIATING

I have asked my friends, colleagues and clients who follow this program to make a list of all of their significant relationships and then identify in which Zone each relationship exists. You can do the same. If most of your relationships are in the Green Zone, you are one of the fortunate. You can now focus on your painful Yellow and Red Zone relationships that are a source of stress in your life.

I am of the opinion that there are three ways you can deal with Yellow and Red Zone relationships and they are by resolving, dissolving or mediating.

To resolve the conflicts of Yellow and Red Zone relationships both parties need to be willing and able to communicate in the Green

Zone. You can talk to them or write a letter inviting them for a heart to heart dialogue.

Sometimes it is fruitful to first write in your diary, putting all your thoughts and feelings on paper before you write the letter to the person concerned. As you write in your diary, you may realize that you have been harboring anger and resentment for your dear ones. After identifying your feelings you are often more able to make a genuine attempt to improve the relationship. You can then write a letter to your dear one and suggest a face-to-face meeting or a response to your letter.

Remember Green Zone dialogue only takes place if both parties are in the Green Zone so that a genuine attempt to resolve your issues is likely to happen.

If the other person is not willing to resolve the conflicts and create a Green Zone relationship, then you may come to the decision

Dr. K. Sohail & Bette Davis

that you need to resolve painful aspects of the relationship or even dissolve the relationship completely. With some personal soul searching you might be able to come to the conclusion that it is best to say goodbye to unhealthy relationships and put your mind at ease and not unnecessarily waste your positive energy in negative relationships.

If you cannot resolve the painful conflicts or dissolve the unhealthy relationships on your own you might request a mediator, either a friend or a therapist to help you. In our clinical practice we have helped dozens of couples resolve their conflicts and save their marriages and friendships.

Green Zone Living

LEARNING TO COMMUNICATE IN THE GREEN ZONE

The first step in communicating effectively and respectfully is recognizing your personal communication style and then noticing what happens when you interact with people who use a different method of communication. I have been observing such interactions, especially in marital therapy sessions.

It has been fascinating to see how women communicate so differently than men. With many couples, I see men talking in a logical and rational manner while women communicate from an emotional perspective. Such a fundamental difference in style can be a source of frustration for either side and can push the communication efforts of the couple into the Yellow Zone. It can then easily sink into the disharmony so common in the Red Zone,

Dr. K. Sohail & Bette Davis

particularly if they are not patient and remain oblivious as to what is occurring emotionally. To bring this issue to the attention of one couple, I wrote the following letter.

Dear Dawn and Solomon,

After being married for 25 years, both of you wonder why you still have problems communicating with each other. Why is it that whenever you try to talk to each other, the dialogue turns into a heated discussion, the discussion into a debate and the debate into an argument. Within no time you get angry, raise your voices and start verbally fighting? At the end of your arguments you are both emotionally bruised and the issue you started to discuss never gets resolved.

You have asked my impression about your different styles of communication and what can be done to improve them. I have listened to you talk with each other and I have talked to you separately. It seems to me that when you talk to me you are different people than when you talk to each other.

Why is that? You are not different from many other couples who come to talk to us. It seems at times as if you belong to separate worlds. Both of you speak the same words but their meaning becomes different when you are listening to them. If someone asked me how both of you communicate, I would say, "Like many men, Solomon speaks the language of the head while Dawn uses emotion and intuition and speaks the language of her heart. Solomon presents the objective point of view while Dawn comes forward with the subjective."

If both of you have the same style there would be no problem. It is interesting that neither of you has communication problems with your friends. It is fascinating to see how each of you perceives the other's style.

Dawn says, "He is not available emotionally."

Dr. K. Sohail & Bette Davis

Solomon says, "She is so overly sentimental, I tune her out."

With such perceptions I am not surprised that both of you feel misunderstood by the other. When I listen to you, I feel as if Dawn is a novelist who likes to share all of the details while Solomon is a short story writer who is very economical and does not want to waste words. Sometimes he even expresses himself telegraphically. That is why he becomes impatient listening to Dawn's detailed descriptions. He wants to know the bottom line and when Dawn does not get to it quickly, he tunes her out and that makes Dawn very frustrated. A couple of times he fell asleep while she was talking. She became so angry she felt like hitting him but instead, and wisely, she went for a long walk to cool down.

I am sharing these impressions so that we can focus on your communication styles when I meet with you next week.

Sincerely,

Sohail

Green Zone Living

Couples who have problems with communication have to learn the differences between the Green Zone and Red Zone style of communication. With those using the Green Zone style of communication there is spontaneous sharing and feedback and the interaction can go on and on comfortably and enjoyably when patience and understanding is used. People who have Green Zone relationships easily resolve conflicts.

In the Yellow Zone style of communication, conflicts emerge, the exchange of sharing and feedback is blocked and tension is created. Differences turn into verbal sparring and if the relationship sinks into the Red Zone, neither party can find the patience and civility to sort out the differences. Often the cooling off period is quite lengthy.

Dr. K. Sohail & Bette Davis

Becoming aware of your communication style in your significant relationships is the first stage to Green Zone communication.

Next is developing the art of constructive communication. It is evident that couples with relationships problems, who live and love in the Yellow and Red Zones have either lost or never developed the art of communicating constructively.

Such couples:

- do not listen to each other,
- do not know how to share their feelings and thoughts effectively as well as respectfully, and
- do not provide constructive feedback.

Therefore one of the basic principles of healthy and fruitful communication - the message given should be the message received - is never undertaken nor understood.

When there is unhealthy communication and the couple feels a need to discuss a serious problem or painful issue, the verbal and non-verbal interactions gradually deteriorate and after minutes, hours or even days of discussion, they have made no headway in their problem resolution. During that process they emotionally bruise each other either verbally or through silence and spend a lot of time licking their wounds, both real and imaginary. Every attempt to make things better seems to make the situation worse.

I emphasize to struggling couples that healthy and constructive communication is possible only when both parties are in their Green Zone. Trying to reason when you are in your Green Zone with someone in the Red Zone is like talking to a drunk person. I emphasize that therapy will help them improve their communication first with me and then later with each other. I work to rectify some of their faulty patterns at two levels.

Experiential:

One spouse talks to me…the other listens

The other spouse talks to me…the first one listens

They both discuss an issue…I listen

I talk…they both listen

Conceptual:

If the couple has difficulty picking up subtle hints, then I try to explain things to them in a simple logical manner, highlighting their communication style and circular interaction. This part is best described as being educational.

Green Zone Living

Example:

A couple wanted to paint a room together. The wife was conscientious but quite the perfectionist, the husband was responsible but carefree and far less exacting. They had the following dialogue in my office:

H: "You are too rigid!"

W: "No, I am not."

H: "Yes, you are. I had no problems painting the room with my brother."

W: "The credit goes to him. You are so lazy. You drive me crazy."

H: "No, I'm not lazy. You're just too rigid."

And so the discussion can go round and round in circles, taking any joy out of their accomplishment and leaving each feeling defensive.

The aim of professional intervention would be to make them aware of their faulty communication pattern and then help them learn constructive approaches, so that at the end of the discussion:

> • they have not emotionally bruised each other
>
> • some decisions have been made
>
> •they feel their discussion was fruitful, and
>
> • they are interested in retaining what they now know and in learning more.

Green Zone communication has a positive cognitive as well as emotional component.

If the communication in my office shows that a couple cannot discuss very many things without emotionally bruising each other I will suggest:

Green Zone Living

- at home they discuss only "neutral" issues and

- bring their emotionally-charged issues to therapy sessions.

In therapy I hope that even if the couples have to "fight" as their way of communicating, they learn how to fight fairly and constructively, much like a sparring match with padded gloves where no hurt is intended.

Circular Thinking

One of the subjects I discuss with couples is the concept of circular thinking. I share with them that in intimate relationships the communication is circular rather than linear. In linear thinking A causes B to happen, and B causes C to happen, and C causes D to occur. In circular thinking, A affects B and then B affects A, and a circular pattern develops in the relationship.

The following clinical example might highlight my point. I once worked in therapy with a couple where the husband had an alcohol problem and his wife was depressed. The husband had been getting help from a psychologist for years with minimum benefit and his wife had been treated by a psychiatrist for years and mainly taking different medications with little improvement. I found it strange that his psychologist had never invited the man's wife for a joint meeting and her psychiatrist had never met the husband. Both were being treated in isolation. After I worked with both spouses together for a few sessions, they realized how her depression and his alcohol problem were emotionally connected. After being introduced to the dynamics of circular thinking they soon realized that:

- the more he drank, the more she withdrew.

Green Zone Living

• the more she withdrew, the more reason he found to go out with his drinking buddies.

• the more he came home drunk, the more justified she felt in holding back her love and affection.

• the more he felt rejected and neglected, the more he went out and got drunk.

• the more he got drunk, the more she withdrew into her depression.

The negative cycle continued for years until it was addressed in joint therapy. What a rewarding experience it was to see how hard they worked to break the negative cycle with their newly learned Green Zone Philosophy and how significant the improvement was in just a few months.

When spouses blame each other and each expects the other to change, they feel helpless when it hasn't happened. I urge them to become part of the solution rather than remaining part of the problem. As each spouse becomes aware of the process which they often do at a different pace, they feel more in control and more optimistic. One spouse feeds on the other's spontaneous reaction to getting into the Green Zone.

Overcoming Common Pitfalls to Communication

If you and your partner are living and loving in the Yellow Zone and experiencing tension in your communication, you might benefit from reviewing how you discuss your problems and resolve your conflicts. In healthy communication, knowing what not to say is as important as knowing what to say. Over the years I have observed that the following characteristics are very detrimental to the relationship. Being aware of those pitfalls helps couples to protect their relationship.

These are mechanisms by which the partner in the Yellow or Red Zone pulls the other, who may well be in the Green Zone, down into the Yellow or Red Zone.

One such mechanism is "taking the bait." The person in the Yellow or Red Zone can become so frustrated or angry that they throw out a comment which becomes the bait that the other cannot resist. In no time, both are battling in the Red Zone either with loud, biting sarcasm or in complete silence. The following are the most common ways spouses throw the bait that they know will provoke a reaction in the other person.

Accusations

Rather than sharing one's feelings by saying "I feel sad" or "I feel hurt" or "I feel disappointed",

Dr. K. Sohail & Bette Davis

the person in the Yellow or Red Zone remarks, often not too gently, "You were so cruel yesterday" or "You offended me last night" or "You insulted me when we visited your parents". When people properly share feelings from the Green Zone, it gives the other person the opportunity to offer support. But when accusations start to fill the air, others become defensive and in many cases start their slide down the slippery slope into the Red Zone. Accusations often become irresistible bait, containing a barbed hook that's hard to remove, and which most people have trouble resisting.

Generalizations

I've met many spouses who, rather than saying to their significant other, "Last night when I was talking to you, you seemed lost in your own world", they tend to jump in with both feet and say accusingly, "You never listen to me" or "You

Green Zone Living

always ignore me" or "You think all women are stupid." Such comments certainly hinder problem solving and in fact often do the opposite. Rather than focusing on a specific incident or behaviour for the purpose of problem solving, they launch such a broad attack on the person's character and attitudes that they can't help but battle back.

Bring up the Past

One sure way of pushing your communications into the Red Zone is to attempt to get the upper hand by raising past sins or omissions. If the grieved one feels they are not getting the type of attention they seek, they may be tempted to remind the other person of their failings in previous instances when the same problem arose. The issue that needs addressing gets lost in a general, usually worthless, rehashing of the problems from the past.

Dr. K. Sohail & Bette Davis

Exploiting Vulnerabilities

Almost everyone has unresolved issues and inevitably, we become aware of these sensitive areas in the personalities of the people we are close to. Unfortunately, those sensitivities can potentially serve as weapons if we choose to exploit them. I call those areas "sore elbows" or "bruised knees." We can be respectful and not touch those areas so that they heal with time or we can push or jab at them, which will elicit a predictable angry response every time. A couple living in the Green Zone respect each other's bruised knees and sore elbows while those in the Red Zone, are compelled to seek out and jab at these sensitivities through subtle hints or even biting sarcasm. Those who are wounded will quickly realize what is happening and complain, "You certainly know how to push my buttons."

Green Zone Living

Becoming aware of a partner's sensitive areas and respecting them is an important step in keeping the relationship in the Green Zone.

If you want to know how other couples brought their relationship into their Green Zone and resolved their conflicts by improving their communication you can read our book, *The Art of Loving in Your Green Zone*. You can also use the following Green Zone Principles that we provide to couples as the basic guiding principles to improving relationships. They are in the form of an agreement since we suggest that they make a joint commitment to honor them.

Our Green Zone Agreement

1. The goal is that both partners and the relationship live in the Green Zone.

2. Green Zone communication is only possible when both partners are in the Green Zone.

3. It is the responsibility of each person to live in the Green Zone and recover from the Yellow/Red Zones.

4. The person who goes to the Yellow/Red Zone announces it to the Green Zone person and then asks to change the subject or to leave temporarily. The Green Zone person gives that time and space to the Yellow/Red Zone person to recover.

5. The Yellow/Red Zone person announces that they are back in the Green Zone.

6. Both partners try to go to bed and sleep in the Green Zone.

7. Both partners start the next day in the Green Zone.

8. If an individual is in the Yellow/Red Zone for other reasons he/she shares that

Green Zone Living

with their partner so that the partner does not feel bad or guilty for unknowingly pushing the other in the Yellow/Red Zone.

9. Weekly *State of the Union Meetings* are held to share good and bad feelings and concerns. *Date Night* is scheduled weekly to build the positive, intimate aspects of the relationship.

10. A couples' journal or letters to each other can be used to keep a record of the mutual growth and the issues resolved.

SIXTH STEP - CREATING GREEN ZONE SYSTEMS

Once people recognize their own Emotional Zones and then are aware of the quality of their relationships, I encourage them next to recognize the systems in which they live. Most people live in numerous systems simultaneously:

♦ Family System

♦ Work System

♦ Social/Community System

I share with people that, like individuals and relationships, human systems also have an individual character and live in different Zones. Recognizing the Zones of each of these systems and one's relationships within them is very important in recognizing the changes in one's Emotional Zones. Systems have a major impact on individuals because, in most cases, systems are more powerful than individuals.

Green Zone Living

Family System

We were all part of a family system as we are growing up and most of us get married and have a family of our own. Fortunate are those who grow up in healthy Green Zone families and are nurtured by their parents. Growing up in a Green Zone family ensures a confident personality with positive self-image, self-worth, and self-confidence. In Green Zone families, people have positive role models and are more likely to have Green Zone relationships in the future.

People who grow up in Yellow and Red Zone families often encounter tension, anxiety and poor communication in their various environments. Those who grow up in the Yellow Zone are chronically anxious, frustrated, angry or sad. They might have managed to acquire a family, a job and even a social circle of

Dr. K. Sohail & Bette Davis

acquaintances, but they lack a general attitude of happiness. It is not uncommon for them to visit the Red Zone by having panic attacks, losing control and having fights with their loved ones or getting so depressed that they feel immobilized. When they continue to exist in the Red Zone, and do not get proper help to deal with painful issues, they get stuck in the Red Zone and are unable to get out on their own. In many cases they need professional help.

Work System

Many people, besides being part of a family system are also part of a work system. It is important for people to recognize the Emotional Zone in which the work system moves. A work system in the Green Zone has a fair and just environment where people feel appreciated and their concerns are taken seriously. In Yellow and Red Zone workplaces people feel like robots.

Green Zone Living

Decisions are made from the top down, for political and economic reasons. There is, too often, a dehumanizing atmosphere. The communication between workers and management often breaks down and conflicts are not resolved.

Due to political and economic changes, many workplaces, which started out in the Green Zone have transformed over the years gradually regressing to the Yellow or Red Zones. In the face of staff cut backs, arbitrary transfers, and the imposition of new technology without adequate training, many employees struggle in vain with increased workloads and other challenges in the workplace. We see many in therapy who have become increasingly frustrated and angry, feeling unenthusiastic and burnt out. People working in such Red Zones suffer from a wide range of physical ailments and emotional problems. Many times suppressed aggression is shown as physical symptoms or what is also referred to as psychosomatic conditions, which includes high blood pressure, irritable bowel syndrome and migraines. Some need intensive psychotherapy to deal with their repressed hostility and on- going stress.

After recognizing that the work system is in the Red Zone some people decide to leave and join a Green Zone System. But if you feel you have no other option but to work in that stressful work environment you can build a circle of colleagues who can support each other and create an Emotional Raincoat so that you are less affected by the toxicity.

It is important to be aware that systems are often emotionally stronger than individuals. Consequently, it is very hard for individuals to be in the Green Zone if the system is in the Red. It is amazing to see how many people find it

Green Zone Living

necessary to take sick leave or short and long term disability in stressful work environments.

In our book *The Art of Working in Your Green Zone,* we have identified different factors that force the work system into the toxic Red Zone. We also discuss what steps workers, union representatives and managers can take to bring the system into the Green Zone. If managers and union leaders are sensitive to the needs of their co-workers they can develop programs to educate their staff and managers about workplace stress. Understanding what it is and what to do about it, is an essential element in building workplaces that are in the Green Zone. Leaders, who themselves emulate a Green Zone Philosophy, are those who appreciate that spending money to prevent burnout in the long run is more advantageous to the organization and the individual than paying huge amounts in medical and sick benefits to try to correct the problem after the fact. Managers and union leaders who work together in cooperation to help their workers create healthy work environments are responsibly managing human and financial resources. If coping with a Red Zone workplace is an issue for you, we suggest you read, *The Art of Working in Your Green Zone.*

Social System

To create a Green Zone Lifestyle it is also important to be aware of all the social organizations and cultural institutions you are involved in and whether they live in the Green, Yellow and Red Zones. As we mentioned, since systems are often emotionally stronger than individuals it is hard to live in the Green Zone if the system you are interacting with is in the Red Zone. It might be wise to find Green Zone Systems that you can enjoy as they will help you grow.

Green Zone Living

SEVENTH STEP - CREATING A GREEN ZONE LIFESTYLE

Over the years I have discovered that there are three paths that lead to a Green Zone Lifestyle. They can unite with each other at different points in life - they are creating, sharing and serving humanity.

For anyone to begin the journey to *creativity*, the first step is to discover a special interest in life. All children enjoy playing but too few adults allow themselves to smile, laugh and be playful, to use humour or to feel an active part of life. The special interest can be related to any aspect of life and can give birth to worthwhile hobbies. Some begin with a visit to a library, pursuing a special sport, or joining friends in special projects. As time passes, these special interests and hobbies will grow to become more meaningful and gradually transform into a passion. Developing that passion, that interest, is the first step to pursuing a dream. The second step is *sharing that special gift* with others.

People with a passion are energized and motivated. They move beyond the mundane activities and relationships we all encounter. It gives them a focus, a sense of direction, a direction that is guided by their hearts rather than traditions. Such freedom leads to happiness and tranquility which blossoms into a newly found peace of mind.

Creativity can be expressed in everyday life, in acts of cooking, baking, knitting, sewing, interior decoration, gardening, creating games with children and the thousands of other activities open to us all. For some, their creativity is expressed in creative arts, whether they be poems, or stories, songs or paintings. Even for those people who suffer from a lot of pain in their hearts, I encourage them to read the biographies of artists like Frieda Kahlo and Vincent Van Gogh who transformed their pains into paintings and writers like Virginia Woolf whose novels are as entertaining as enlightening. These artists gradually realized that their hardships provided them with raw material for their masterpieces. When suffering finds a meaning it no longer remains an affliction, it transforms into a work of art.

It has been my observation that many Creative Personalities whether poets or philosophers, musicians or painters like to visit the Yellow and Red Zones to get raw material and then come back to the Green Zone to create their masterpieces. Those who cannot come back from the Yellow and Red Zones suffer from emotional problems and may ultimately have a nervous breakdown needing help from the mental health professionals to get back to their Green Zone.

Green Zone Living

Over the centuries, scientists, artists, mystics and social reformers have used their creativity to *serve humanity* thus playing a significant role in the evolution of humanity. Creative people are in the minority but they lead the majority, inspiring them to get in touch with their own creativity. They are then able to share with others and serve their own communities, in particular and humanity, in general. One such example was a mystic poet Walt Whitman, who offered his services at Soldiers Hospital in Washington during the American Civil War in the 1800s. A friend wrote about one of his visits to the hospital, " Never shall I forget that visit…to one he gave a few words of cheer, for another he wrote a letter home, to others he gave an orange, a few comits [sugar confection], a cigar, a pipe and tobacco, a sheet of paper, or a postage stamp, all of which, and many other things, were in his capacious haversack…he did the things for them which no nurse or doctor could do, and he seemed to leave a benediction at every cot as he passed along. The doctors said he performed miracles, miracles of healing.

Many of the soldiers remembered him years later as 'the man with the face of a saviour'. Walt Whitman wrote a beautiful poem describing his feeling at the sight of a slain enemy.

> For my enemy is dead, a man divine as myself is dead
> I look where he lies white-faced and stiff in the coffin...I draw near
> Bend down and touch lightly with my lips the white face in the coffin.

Walt Whitman, like many other humanists, helps us see a human being even in our enemy.

When we read the biographies of scientists, artists, mystics and social reformers, we find that they had discovered their Green Zone. They continually sacrificed because they believed in their dream, their goal, and their mission. Nelson Mandela, who lived for years in a prison on Robin Island in South Africa, transformed it into a Green Zone, an island of peace and hope surrounded by an ocean of ignorance, poverty, prejudice and suffering. He dealt with his problems gracefully. That is why, in spite of all that he faced, he never became bitter.

People who can transform their Green Zones into Green Islands, like Canadian Terry Fox, India's Mother Teresa, America's Martin Luther King Jr. and South Africa's Nelson Mandela, discover the secret of living peacefully in their hearts and serving humanity the best way they can. I present those people as role models to all those who do not have positive and inspiring role models in their own families and communities.

Discovering our Green Zone Lifestyle helps us to grow stronger as individuals while we are serving our communities doing voluntary work. It helps us make our tomorrows better than our yesterdays.

Green Zone Living

Chapter Two

CREATING A GREEN ZONE WORLD

If we would like to raise Green Zone children, then we have to provide them Green Zone families, schools and communities. Those three systems have to work together to ensure that all the needs of the children are met. If there are conflicts between those systems, they need to be resolved gracefully, respectfully and peacefully as the adults representing those systems are the role-models for the next generation. Folk wisdom has taught us that it takes a whole village to raise a child.

Green Zone Families

The family system is the first system that children experience when they come to this world. That system passes on the values and traditions from one generation to the next. The family system is tied with invisible threads on the one hand to individuals and on the other hand to the community. When children are raised in happy and healthy Green Zone families then it is easier for them to become part of Green Zone schools.

Green Zone Schools

The school system tries to continue the growth promoting process that families had started at home. A Green Zone school system not only helps children get in touch with their academic potential but also prepares them to work and serve humanity thus becoming an integral part of the Green Zone community.

Dr. K. Sohail & Bette Davis

Green Zone Communities

A Green Zone community is based on humanistic principles in which all citizens enjoy equal opportunities, rights and privileges irrespective of the religious, ethnic, gender and class differences. A Green Zone community supports Green Zone families and schools so that Green Zone children grow up to become Green Zone adults and prepare the healthy and happy foundation for the next generation.

We are all aware that those children who are exposed to neglect and abuse in Red Zone families, schools and communities have a tendency to either suffer due to serious emotional problems or become delinquent and get involved in the cycle of violence. That cycle of violence can go on from one generation to another and increase emotional and social suffering.

Green Zone Living

To decrease human suffering and create an environment in which people from all walks of life can live and grow together, we need to think and work together to create Green Zone families, schools and communities for our children as they are our hopes and dreams of a Green Zone future. If we raised them in Red Zone environments, I am afraid our dreams might turn into nightmares.

Dr. K. Sohail & Bette Davis

GREEN ZONE HUMANISTIC PHILOSOPHY

I have gradually come to realize that the world we live in and the dilemmas we face as human beings today are quite complex. I strongly feel that before pointing our fingers at others we have to acknowledge that we are our own worst enemies. We fall into the same traps of biases and prejudices as we accuse others. I think that we have reached a turning point in history where we are being forced to make certain choices.

I hope that we do not proceed on the path of self-destruction, ending in collective suicide and instead, decide to embrace new ways of living harmoniously with ourselves, other human beings and Mother Nature. Perhaps one day we will reach that state of communal growth and human evolution where we can accept that whether they are children or elderly, women or minorities, physically disabled or mentally sick,

Green Zone Living

all human beings have a right to live respectfully and grow peacefully. For our future development as a species we have to transcend the resentments based on class, race, gender, language or religious differences. We need to let go of the anger of conflicts between East and West, North and South, first and third world and many other man-made divisions. Sooner or later we have to accept that we are all human, members of the same family and our enemies are part of us, just distant cousins.

I am quite aware that these are my personal and global dreams, but I believe that we are the product of our dreams. When our dreams are shattered we start to disintegrate individually and collectively.

Dr. K. Sohail & Bette Davis

LIFE IS LIKE A RIVER, LET IT FLOW

After forty years of reflection, introspection and contemplation, I have come to this realization that there is a duality in human personality. On the one hand we are our worst enemies but on the other hand we can also become our best friends. Over the centuries we have been evolving and growing as human beings trying to become fully human by raising our personal and social consciousness. We are involved in discovering the laws of nature whether biological or psychological, social or political, creative or cultural. The more we discover those laws the more we develop insights into life and become masters of our destinies. Then we are able to decrease human suffering and increase our chances of leading happy, healthy and peaceful lives.

Green Zone Living

When I reflect upon my personal, creative and professional lives as a physician, psychotherapist, poet and humanist, I realize that one of the insights I have discovered is that life is like a river. As far as the river keeps on flowing the water remains unclean and unhealthy, but when a part of the river stagnates and turns into a pond, it becomes infected and unhealthy.

My first awareness of that truth was as a physician. In my clinical practice I discovered that physical illnesses and human sufferings are often because of the stoppage or slowing down of the flow in a particular bodily system.

In the cardiovascular system, if the blood stops flowing from the heart to the blood vessels to body organs, then there are health problems in the form of oxygen deprivation and heart attack or clots in blood vessels causing death of an organ or the person.

Dr. K. Sohail & Bette Davis

We can see a similar mechanism in other systems of the body:

- blockage in the gastro- intestinal system can cause abdominal pain and intestinal obstruction
- narrowing of the wind pipe in the respiratory system can decrease the flow of oxygen leading to respiratory distress and
- diminishing the flow of an electrical current from the brain to the nerves to the organs can lead to numbness and paralysis.

As a physician it was my responsibility to find out which system was blocked and what could be done to let the system flow smoothly and restore health. I was aware that if that flow was not restored promptly with change of nutrition, exercise and medications, it might need a surgical intervention to overcome the obstruction.

Green Zone Living

When I became a psychotherapist I discovered the same principle operating in mental health. I found out that healthy people had a free flow of emotions and could share and express their feelings freely. If this expression was blocked and people suppress or repress their feelings because they were painful, then those feelings turned into anger and resentment, anxiety and depression, jealousy and paranoia. I share with my patients that they need to learn to let those feelings flow like a river to stay healthy, otherwise those suppressed and repressed feelings can cause emotional problems and mental illness. Those patients who have a hard time sharing their feelings verbally because of their shyness or embarrassment are encouraged to write them down in their diary, which is another way of emotional expression. Those people who suppress and repress their feelings for a long time get so sick that they need hospitalization and treatment with medications.

As a poet I also became aware that many artists act like community therapists. In their poems and plays and paintings they express the painful feelings of their community and represent those people who cannot express their own emotions. That is why it is very crucial for a healthy community to have freedom of speech so that writers and artists can freely express themselves. Those communities, who put their poets in jail or their philosophers in exile, set the stage for an unhealthy society. Poets and philosophers need not be persecuted or executed as they keep the river of life flowing.

As a humanist I discovered that those countries and communities remain healthy who let their resources keep on flowing like a river. When a small group of people become greedy, start hoarding wealth and economic resources,

Green Zone Living

the social and political system starts to stagnate and within a few years or decades we see a big discrepancy between the rich and the poor and people suffer. In some communities the minority holds the power and deprives the majority of their basic rights, in other communities the majority holds the power and deprives the minority of their human rights. Whether it is the minority or majority, if economic wealth and social privileges are not shared by all members of the community, the society stagnates and the system stops flowing freely. In such communities people's education and health care becomes scarce and people start to suffer. If that happens then reformers and revolutionaries of that community identify the problem and try their best to channel the energies of their community. They realize that if people do not have their basic rights and do not live with respect and dignity, they are likely to get so frustrated that they become violent and destructive which will increase human suffering.

When I read their biographies, reformers reminded me of physicians, and revolutionaries of surgeons. They try to help their communities heal but enlightened leaders know how to use their power wisely. They are aware that to keep the river of life flowing we need to address the needs of people from all classes and cultures.

I have also realized that at an international level we need organizations that make sure that power is not held in the hands of a small group of powerful countries and rich communities in which others do not have veto power, otherwise the flow of power and wealth will stagnate and weaker communities and countries will suffer.

I have come to the realization that all of us are connected with each other like different parts of the human body or the links of a chain, we could say we are all part of the chain of life. And we know that the chain is only as strong as its weakest link. Those communities that are not caring and compassionate towards their weakest members - the sick and the disabled - deteriorate over time. Sharing keeps the river of caring flowing freely. Democratic and secular societies have discovered the secret of sharing the power. They try their best to ensure that the political power does not stay with one person or one party for very long because they know that stagnation of power can corrupt and absolute power can corrupt absolutely. When the powerful start sharing the economic and political power with the less empowered, only then will the river of life flow freely.

Those individuals, families and communities, who know this secret share their love and affection with their friends and relatives, their wealth and resources with other communities and countries and their knowledge and wisdom with the future generations so that they can lead a happy, healthy and peaceful life. They realize that we are all mysteriously connected to each other and our future evolution, growth and progress depends upon the secret of the river of life flowing. If we do not see all human beings as part of humanity and only focus on our own tribe, whether based on class or race, religion or language, history or geography, gender or nationalism, then we will obstruct the flow of river of life and increase human suffering sooner or later.

In the 21st century, humanity is at a crossroads. I hope rather than choosing the road of self-destruction we choose the road of sharing our resources with the whole of humanity and not restrict it only for our own community and country. I dream of a world in which the rich will be sharing with the poor, the stronger will be

Green Zone Living

sharing with the weaker and the powerful will be sharing with the most vulnerable. I dream of a day when we let the river of life flow physically as well as emotionally, economically as well as politically, nationally as well as internationally with caring and compassion so that we can all grow and evolve and become fully human.

Dr. K. Sohail & Bette Davis

GREEN ZONE PHILOSOPHY IS LIKE A MUSICAL INSTRUMENT

When people ask me what kind of creative product Green Zone Philosophy is, I share with them that in my opinion creative products are of two kinds.

The first kind of a creative product is a song that an artist writes and sings. Let us take the example of Kenny Roger's famous song *The Gambler*. After it was written, composed and recorded, it must have been sung and played hundreds, thousands even millions of times. But each time the singer sings the same lyrics and plays the same tune. Even Kenny Rogers, the creator, does not change it.

The second type of creative product is a musical instrument. The artists who created the fiddle or guitar or piano, created a musical instrument. Such an instrument does not dictate or demand what to play on the instrument. One musician can play Classical music, the other Jazz and yet another Rock and Roll. Once the musicians learn the basics of the instrument they can play any composition or melody on it.

For me the Green Zone Philosophy is more like a musical instrument than a song. Once people learn the basics of the philosophy they can modify and improvise it to play their own tune and express their own inner music. And when people learn to express and share their inner music and identify their hidden potential, that life has offered them, they can learn the art of leading a happy, healthy and peaceful life.

I share with my friends, clients and colleagues that I practice my Green Zone Philosophy everyday and share my music with others by creating my Green Zone Lifestyle. I encourage others to create their own Green Zone Lifestyle. The Green Zone Philosophy is so flexible that it accommodates every person's uniqueness.

For me the Green Zone Philosophy is my creative expression, my work of art and my gift of love to serve humanity. It helps people to express and share their inner music.

A few years ago I wrote a short poem titled

APPREHENSION

I am afraid
The noise of the outside world
Will drown one day
The music inside

I do not want people's music to drown and my Green Zone Philosophy is my humble attempt to inspire people to cherish their music themselves and then share it with others.

I believe every child is born with a special gift and a special music and it is the

Green Zone Living

responsibility of parents, grandparents, aunts, uncles and teachers to recognize that music and talent and help the child learn a musical instrument so that he/she can share his/her music with the world. First the child learns to play solo and then learns to play with other human beings and we create a human orchestra that inspires others and helps them grow. Those children who were successful in discovering their talent and inner music became scientists and artists and philosophers and reformers and revolutionaries and played their role in human evolution.

I believe that when the music of children is suppressed and oppressed and they are silenced by autocratic families and schools and oppressive communities, then it creates stress and those children suffer as adults. Finally that suppressed music explodes in the form of cries and screams and the melodious music turns violent and people have breakdowns. I share with those people who have suffered for a long time that once they would recognize their potential and their inner music that has been suppressed, they can unlearn the negative conditioning. I share with them my own Green Zone Story and ask them to read the Green Zone Stories of other people who benefited from the Green Zone Philosophy and transformed their lives. I reassure them that once they get inspired and get in touch with their suppressed talent and hidden music they can transform their breakdown into a breakthrough. I feel honored when people write to me and share with me their wonderful encounters with the Green Zone Philosophy and narrate their Green Zone Story. To inspire others I am collecting these stories on our website www.greenzoneliving.ca and some of them are included later in this book.

Green Zone Living

Chapter Three

THE SEVEN STEPS TO MY GREEN ZONE
– A PERSONAL JOURNEY

Dear Dr. Sohail,

When I first came to see you, I had a lot of "Red Zone" things going on in my life. My work life was a huge mess. I had a lot of difficulty in my work relationships with colleagues and administration. Being a high school teacher, I also had to deal with difficult students and difficult parents on top of not getting along with my vice-principal and principal. I was also tired of being used by certain colleagues, expecting me to take on their work as well as my own. This stress at work caused tension at home between me and my husband. Our usual happy-go-lucky relationship was deteriorating quickly, and our marriage was full of insults, sarcasm, and hate. This took a toll on our children, and one son in particular, stuck in the middle with no way out, began venting his own feelings of anger by harming other children at school, swearing at his teachers, and threatening to kill himself. This son, who was only eleven at the time, made life difficult for his two brothers, and even more so for me. This strained relationship with my son, led to a very verbally abusive relationship with my mother, who I never really got along with anyway. So now things with her were even worse than before. I dealt with these poor relationships by complaining and crying to the people who I did have good relationships with, which ended up putting strain and tension on those good relationships, causing them to become "Red" as well. I also liked to shop a lot to make myself feel better, which led to financial worries that I had to deal with too. Nothing was going right in my life when I first came to see you. However, very soon after reading your book, *The Art of Living in your Green Zone*, I began to feel as if there was some hope for me.

With the first step, becoming aware of my *Emotional Zones*, what I had to learn was which "colour" I was feeling, whether "Red", "Yellow", or "Green". I learned quickly that Green is basically any feeling that is positive and makes you feel good. Feeling Yellow meant that I was getting frustrated, annoyed, and was on the verge of raising my voice and saying nasty, hurtful things to people. For me, Red meant that I was absolutely being abusive to people verbally, that I couldn't carry on a conversation without yelling, screaming, insulting, hurting, or taking cheap shots at people. It meant that I was completely pissed off or depressed, lonely, in

Green Zone Living

despair, and not able to function in any way at all. Once I learned these colours of emotion, I was able to identify easily what colour I was experiencing at any given time. In the beginning of our sessions, I was always feeling Yellow or Red, which to me was ok, because at least I was now conscious of what type of emotion I was experiencing. It also helped that you asked me to keep track of my emotional colours throughout the day in a diary.

The second step, *recognizing changes in my Emotional Zones*, was also easy for me to pick up on, as it was simple to figure out when I became Yellow or Red, what things pushed me into those colours, what, or who, made me feel Yellow, and when did Yellow change to Red. Certain things came to my mind right away. When I walked through the door after a long day of work, I was always bombarded with information from my husband or the kids needing something. Usually

I'd be dealing with phone messages, signing agendas, reading notes, being asked when supper would be ready, and somebody wanting me to drive them somewhere, all before I put my bag down and took my coat off. It made me feel overwhelmed, frustrated, and angry when that happened; all Red Zone feelings.

In order to get out of the Yellow and Red Zones, I had to experience what it might be like to be in the Green Zone. So in the third step, *recovering from my Yellow and Red Zones*, I had to figure out what things made me feel Green - happy, excited, joyful, pleased, relaxed, and so on. And then I had to actually do those Green Zone activities. For example, I had told you that spending quiet time alone, doing something for myself would make me feel relaxed, calm, and energized. You then gave me homework - spend one hour every evening for a month by myself, doing something that made me feel good. At first,

Green Zone Living

this seemed impossible. How would I be able to get a whole hour to myself with a husband who works evenings and three children at home who needed help with homework, uniforms washed, supper made, and fights to be broken up? Not to mention the marking and other work related stuff that had to be done for the next day. But I found a way to make time to be in my Green Zone. At first I wasn't able to do an entire hour, but I eventually got to that point. An hour a day in the Green Zone eventually led to an afternoon in the Green Zone, then a whole day, and then a whole week. After a few months, and with a few other strategies, I was able to spend two whole weeks in the Green Zone, feeling happy, comfortable, rested, able, strong, and confident. I was able to have positive interactions and conversations with people! It felt great being Green for that long! Once I knew how to get into my Green Zone, I needed ways to stay there.

Dr. K. Sohail & Bette Davis

The fourth step, *restraining from going to the Yellow and Red*, was challenging. It required me to deal with Yellow and Red Zone people and situations, while remaining in the Green. This was difficult, especially if the other people I was dealing with did not know about the colours of emotion. I had to think of things that would bring me back to the Green if I did slip into Yellow and Red with other people. One thing I came up with was that it would be ok to say to someone that I would get back to them at a later time. So, for example, if my colleague needed me to do them a favour that would require a lot of time, effort, and energy that I didn't want to invest, usually I would have become very upset, uncomfortable, I would have felt like I was being used and that this colleague was a lazy so-and-so who could go to you-know-where, because I had enough "favours" that I had to do for myself. But Step Four taught me that instead, I could say,

"I'll think about it and get back to you later." By saying this, I bought myself time to calm down, think rationally, and come back to them in a more positive mood, with a confident answer that would state clearly what I was able, or not able, to do for them. Step Four was eventually a lot easier once I started telling the people in my life what the colours of emotion were and what they meant.

Step Five, *creating Green Zone relationships*, came with mixed reactions. In this step, I was to tell the people in my life about the Green, Yellow, and Red Zones. This would help to create Green Zone relationships between me and the important people in my life. It meant that I would have to tell them about my therapy and how I now communicated and thought about feelings. This was fine when it came to my family, because they knew I was seeing you and that I was trying something new. The terms "Red",

"Yellow", and "Green" became the new language used in my home with my children, husband, brother, and parents. Whenever one of us was feeling a certain way, the colours would come up to describe that feeling. For example, when I become overwhelmed now when first walking into the house, I just tell the kids, that "Mommy's feeling a little Yellow right now, could you come back to me when my coat is off, and my bag is away? I'll be Green by then. Thanks". Quite often I'll also hear one of my kids say to another, "You're making me feel "Red" and I don't like it!" So, it's working at home. Creating colour language at work was a little harder for me, and so I only made it known to one or two people who I trust, feel comfortable with, and who I knew would appreciate the concept and this has created Green Zone relationships with them as well. There are other

Green Zone Living

people at work who I have not shared the colour zones concept with, which led me to Step Six.

Step Six is all about creating *Green Zone systems with your family, your work, and within your community*. Some systems, as mentioned before, are easy to do this with, and others are not so easy. For those systems or people who I cannot create a Green Zone relationship with, either because I am not comfortable, or they are not willing, I try to remember to wear my Emotional Raincoat. So for example, I do not get along well with my principal at work. But I also do not have to interact with him on a regular basis, so it is not a relationship I would consider making Green by telling him about the colours of emotion. Instead, every time I must interact with him, I walk into the potentially Red situation and/or conversation feeling Green and wearing an imaginary raincoat (or in this case, an imaginary suit of armor) that will "protect" me from any

Red things he may say or do. This suit of armor acts as my shield against any Red attacks that may come my way. This allows me to hear what he is saying without becoming Red. It also allows me to respond to him in a Green manner and leave the situation still feeling Green, and not allow him to affect how I feel in a major way. Sometimes, it is hard to wear the suit of armor or raincoat, and even though you may walk in wearing it, it somehow is not the right size, and ends up coming off, exposing you to the Red environment, and getting you covered in Red feelings. When this happens, I deal with it by accepting it. There are times when I have gone into a situation feeling Green, and my suit of armor has not worked, and so I come out feeling Red. In this case, I accept that I have felt some negative feelings, or thought some negative thoughts, or even reacted in a negative way, but I do not stay negative. I try to drive through the

Green Zone Living

Red Zone instead of parking in it and staying that way. I have had to do that many times. Drive through the Yellow and Red Zones, but always make a U-turn back to the Green Zone. I believe this is healthy. It becomes unhealthy when I park in Red and stay there overnight.

The seventh step is the final step to following your colours of emotion concept. The seventh step is one that I am still currently working on, and will probably work on for the rest of my life. It requires me to create a *Green Zone lifestyle*. It means I will try to live in the Green Zone for the rest of my life while trying to serve the world in a peaceful, Green Zone way. For me, it means that I will try to set an example for other people by living Green. It means interacting with others in a Green way, seeing the world in a Green way, and contributing to my family, my work, and my community in a Green way. This can be difficult because it requires a constant effort in the beginning to always be aware of living in the Green, but as time goes on, it seems to get easier and easier. I'm finding that the more I feel Green, the more I act Green, and so the more I live Green, which shows in everything I do.

When I first came to you for help, I was in a very Red place. It was so Red, it was almost black. The relationships in my life were crumbling, my work was falling apart, my finances were melting into a sea of debt, my mood was negative, my behaviour was abusive, and my children were becoming what I had become: desperate, lonely, depressed, and in despair. And within a very short amount of time, with your help, I was able to understand and work through my troubles in just seven little steps. For that, Dr. Sohail, I will never be able to repay you, except to promise you that I will carry on your concept of the Red, Yellow, and Green

Green Zone Living

Zones for the rest of my life, passing it on to my students and my children, who will hopefully, one day, live Green too, making the world just a little more Green; and it's all because of you.

With great thanks,

Michelle

Chapter Four

GREEN ZONE STORIES

When Bette was creating our Green Zone Website, she wanted to ask people who had read and benefited from our Green Zone books to share their stories. Not surprisingly, this segment of the website was called *Green Zone Stories*. She thought it would be a good idea to begin this segment with her story as well as my story, so that others can see how the creators of the Green Zone Philosophy practice it in their own life. These are our stories, followed by some of the people who so kindly offered to share their journey.

Green Zone Living

Sohail's Green Zone Story

I feel very fortunate that I have not only been able to discover my Green Zone but also be able to live in it. I still remember those days when I lived in my Yellow Zone and visited Red Zone frequently. Those were the days when I felt quite frustrated, angry and unhappy even resentful and bitter.

I used to be angry with

- ~ myself
- ~ my mother
- ~ my motherland
- ~ my community and
- ~ my culture.

I was resentful that I was born at the wrong place and at the wrong time. I was bitter that I had no choice but to live in my traditional, conservative and religious suffocating environment for more than twenty years. I was unhappy because I saw no hope of resolving my conflicts with my community and my country.

The only option I saw was to leave my home and homeland and discover a new homeland where I could feel free to create a new lifestyle of my own liking. So I moved to Canada, studied psychiatry and became a psychotherapist and a writer.

Over the years my anger and resentment have subsided and my bitterness has dissolved. I discovered my Green Zone Philosophy and by practicing it started living a happy, healthy and peaceful lifestyle. But that transition was a slow process. I was like the turtle of the mythological folktale, which was slow and steady but finally won the race. I remember the times when I used to visit my Green Zone for short periods of time and go back to my Yellow Zone. But then I started spending more and more time and then finally started living in my Green Zone. Now

Green Zone Living

when I am pushed to the Red Zone by stressful environments, I have learnt to drive through and come back to my Green Zone rather than parking in the Red Zone.

I am well aware that it is not humanly possible for all of us to be always living in the Green Zone, as we can be surrounded by Red Zone people and situations from time to time, but we all need to learn ways to cope with them to the best of our ability. I feel fortunate that I have been able to create a Green Island in the Red Sea of the 21st century world that we all live in. If I have to meet a Red Zone Person or enter a Red Zone System in my professional or social lives, I have learnt to wear an Emotional Raincoat so that I am least affected by the toxicity of the environment.

Every morning when I wake up, I look in the mirror, kiss myself and say, "I will try my best to create a happy, healthy and peaceful

Dr. K. Sohail & Bette Davis

Green Zone Day. Maybe this is the last day of my life." Then I plan my day which usually includes,

~   going to work

~   socializing with family and friends and

~   doing some creative work by reading and writing.

At the end of the day when I go to bed, I ask myself, "Did I spend a Green Zone Day?" and when I find the answer "Yes", I feel relaxed and happy. I am glad to be able to

~   serve a few people and help them with their emotional problems

~   have fun with my dear ones and

~   create a few lines.

Before I go to sleep, I say to myself, "If I die tonight I don't want to be angry with anyone. I forgive the people who have wronged me. They have to deal with their own conscience. As far as my own life is concerned I feel proud that I did the best I could." After saying that it does not

Green Zone Living

take me long to fall asleep hoping that if I die I will have a peaceful death.

The next day when I wake up I feel pleased that life has offered me another opportunity to:

~ live a little more

~ learn a little more

~ love a little more

~ dream a little more

~ create a little more

~ serve a little more and

~ make this world a better place to live.

Living in the Green Zone has been a wonderful experience for me. In the last few years I have tried to resolve and dissolve my conflicts with my dear ones, so all my significant relationships are in the Green Zone. I love socializing with them as we bring out the best in each other and I can be my natural self in their company. I am

Dr. K. Sohail & Bette Davis

also lucky to be able to create my Green Zone family, work and social environments and enjoy working and socializing with people I respect. If any problem arises I feel confident that I would be able to resolve or dissolve the conflicts.

So at the age of sixty, I am able to have a Green Zone Lifestyle in which I am able to live, learn, love, dream, create and serve everyday and lead a happy, healthy and peaceful lifestyle. I create my Green Zone Day everyday and I hope I keep on creating it till the day I die.

Bette's Green Zone Story

When Sohail introduced me to the Green Zone model in 2001, I was personally intrigued and instantly aware of the potential use in therapy. So for several months after I read the book, I discussed the concept with Sohail as well as other friends and colleagues and began using it in my own life. "It's simple, like many brilliant

Green Zone Living

concepts, just think of the traffic lights," I thought, "Green means go forward, Yellow means caution, slow down and Red means stop."

One of the first elements that stood out was the concept that while I could be feeling really good in the Green Zone the person next to me may be in distress in the Yellow or Red Zone. I became aware that checking for which Zone I was in first and then which Zone others were in was a wise first step in deciding when and how I would talk to a friend, family or colleague about a troubling or even a pleasant issue. I began more and more to use the Zones as a way of measuring the emotional temperature of a relationship or situation.

As I became more tuned into what Zone I or another person was in, I began to appreciate that a relationship can be in one of those Zones and as well, a system can be in either of the three Zones. The main systems that affect our lives are family, work and social. I was already aware that systems are often more powerful than the individual because, of course, there is power in numbers. This new awareness helped me be more realistic in approaching or working with Yellow or Red Zone systems. I also became more thorough in my planning to interact in those systems. It became my catchphrase that it *is wise, not weak*, to delay addressing a concern with a person or system that is temporarily in the Red Zone until the storm has passed. With a person or system that seemed to be permanently in the Yellow or Red, I was aware that it took some planning to decide how I would deal with them. I also began asking myself whether it was really necessary to deal with some of these persistently Red Zone situations, and if it wasn't, I didn't. I became increasingly more convinced that healthy communication is possible only in the Green Zone.

Green Zone Living

As part of integrating it into my personal life I introduced it to my daughter Adriana one day while we were waiting at the traffic lights. Although she was only eleven years old at the time, her passion for driving anything with wheels and a motor had been developed a couple of years previously when she first sat on a ride-on lawn mower. So she was listening carefully when I started talking about the traffic lights and her interest did not wane when I introduced the concept of Emotional Zones. We both liked the respectful language of the model. Several days later at the end of a very long but Green day, we found ourselves talking about an unpleasant issue and realized that we were both tired. Adriana quickly took advantage of her newfound knowledge and said with a smile, "Mom, I think you're going into the Yellow!" We both laughed and changed the subject but realized that we had discovered a non-escalating

Dr. K. Sohail & Bette Davis

way to give each other feedback about the emotional temperature of our relationship.

Using the model made us more aware when a situation was becoming tense, and on those occasions we no longer wasted emotional energy, trying to find a sensitive way of saying that our interaction was off track. You see I believe that healthy families find ways of communicating in shorthand, ways of conveying a message quickly which can be discussed later when there is more time and I was realizing that the Green Zone Model was a type of shorthand. For example, my daughter received a phone call from her friend, Kristen, when I called her to the phone, she said, "Mom, Kristen and I are in the Yellow. I'm not ready to talk to her yet." Announcing that you're in the Yellow or Red is a good way to put your loved ones on alert so that they can be more sensitive.

Green Zone Living

So as I became excited about the impact of the Green Zone philosophy on my daughter's and my life, I was eager to introduce it to my clients. Their response was as enthusiastic as ours. I found many embraced the concept and were quickly able to apply it to their lives.

Then awhile ago I had the privilege of offering a six week Green Zone seminar to senior high school students and was pleasantly surprised at the ease with which they began using the language and integrating it into their day-to-day experiences. Along with learning about their feelings they were able to have fun with it as well. I had made a comment and that some people are so familiar with living in the Red Zone that they often became permanent residents there and have a condominium, even a subdivision in the Red Zone. When I asked one student who had a good sense of humor, what Zone he felt he lived in, he smiled mischievously

Dr. K. Sohail & Bette Davis

and said that he had a house in the Green Zone but that he had a summer cottage in the Yellow! I also noticed that individuals who were dealing with boundary issues, such as survivors of childhood abuse or those from enmeshed families, embraced it quickly. Gradually they could see how certain situations, issues or people pushed them into the Yellow or Red. For them building their awareness of boundaries was significantly strengthened by the Green Zone model. Their awareness increased over time as they worked on becoming attentive to the boundaries between the Green Zone and the Yellow Zone as well as between the Yellow Zone and the Red Zone.

Around that time my daughter and I had an experience while on vacation which would become a metaphor for emphasizing those invisible boundaries that are important in all of our lives. When we arrived at the airport at the end of a vacation, Adriana, eager to get a cart for our luggage said her goodbyes quickly. After loading the cart she headed toward the door to the airport while I did my final goodbyes with our friends at the curb. She stopped about 10 to15 feet from the door of the airport to wait for me. As she stood waiting, looking back in my direction she moved the luggage cart back and forth similar to the way one would rock a baby carriage. Unbeknownst to Adriana each time she moved the cart forward she would cross an invisible barrier which caused the door of the airport to open, when she wheeled it back the door would close. Of course, therapists love moments like this because they are familiar to many people and can be used to convey a psychological concept. So I now use this story to make the invisible boundaries between each of the Emotional Zones more visible.

Dr. K. Sohail & Bette Davis

Initially the boundary between Zones moves from an invisible boundary that is unknowingly crossed to a speed bump that gets a little more of our attention. And from a speed bump to a wall that increasingly gets higher so that crossing into the next Zone is more in our awareness and more in our control. As one of my clients said, "I know now when my little toe is in the Yellow and I'm choosing not to go there!"

After a couple of months using the Green Zone Model I was really excited about the awareness that I and others were developing. Then the question was, "what to do with all that awareness?" The natural answer was to use it to address the issues that are pushing you out of your Green Zone. Obviously, awareness of the issues, people or situations that cause you distress is very valuable but real emotional strength comes from addressing these challenges.

Green Zone Living

As a therapist I find that people mainly need to learn awareness of their Emotional Zones and usually they need to gain clarity about challenging issues but they can often identify the challenges well. As the analogy goes they may have swept some of these issues under the rug and need prompting to drag them out but usually the awareness of the issue is there. Most people sweep troublesome issues under the rug because they have difficulty resolving them and it can be very stressful to keep reviewing unfinished problems. But what people don't realize is that it requires emotional energy to keep these unresolved issues hidden or to repeatedly put them back in their place, when others push our buttons. As well when these things that are unresolved rear their ugly heads, it is often to our embarrassment.

One of my favorite concepts in *The Art of Living in Your Green Zone* is the discussion around our choices in dealing with stressful, pushing-us-into-the-Red-Zone issues. We can either

    1) resolve or

    2) dissolve; that is we can either address the issue so that it is no longer a problem or if that is not possible, you can dissolve the problem, in other words, end the relationship, change jobs, etc. I find that one of the biggest sources of ongoing stress for people is that they neither resolve nor dissolve problems but continue, some times for years, sitting on the fence between these two options. I jokingly say that sitting on the fence is very uncomfortable because those pickets are sharp! We work really hard in therapy to help people down off the fence and, of course, our first choice is always resolution of an issue rather than dissolving it by ending the relationship or job.

Green Zone Living

Let me give you a personal example of how I got down off the fence in one of the most important relationships in my life – my relationship with my mother. If you saw my Mom and me together these days you would think we had a relationship that was bright Green and yet it wasn't always that way.

It had occurred to me that we had issues that were in all three Zones. When we discussed those that were in the Green we were happy and enjoyed each other's company but when we focused on Yellow Zone issues we quickly moved to the Red and felt frustrated and distressed. I began to look at all of these issues and realized that if we had 15 issues we regularly discussed, 7 of them were in the Red. 3 were in the Yellow and 5 in the Green. I approached my Mom and explained this. She had met Sohail many years ago and was very fond of his sense of humor and pleasant nature, so she was quite

Dr. K. Sohail & Bette Davis

open to reading *The Art of Living in Your Green Zone*. I said that clearly the issues in the Green Zone were good, and asked her if we could resolve the Yellow Zone issues to bring them to the Green. We were able to do that and even found a couple of Red Zone issues we could resolve. So now we have a number of issues that we feel really good about. If either of us gets into a Yellow or Red Zone issue, we usually choose one of these three ways of handling it:

1) be quiet for awhile to let the other person clue into what Zone they are in;

2) make a brief comment to correct the course such as, "Let's not get into that. I think that's going to get us in to the Yellow Zone." or

3) if all else fails, gracefully end the conversation and reconnect when both are in the Green Zone again.

Green Zone Living

I have derived so many benefits from using the Green Zone concept and I know a number of friends, family members and clients have as well. It is an easy to use concept that we have integrated into our professional interactions with colleagues and clients, and also into our personal lives. At home we are a Green Zone family and at work we are a Green Zone clinic. I am delighted with its significant impact on my personal growth. Embracing the Green Zone Philosophy has enhanced my relationships and the ease with which I handle even difficult, Red Zone situations.

Dr. K. Sohail & Bette Davis

Chris' Green Zone Story

From Reds and Wrongs to Greens and Rights

Anxiety is something I've had since I was about two years old, feeling pressure all my life. Raised by parents that thought they were doing the right thing, but weren't. My father served 4 years in World War 2 which destroyed his life. I think the stress he suffered in the war rubbed off on me as a kid. My mother's mother was a neurotic worrier, which I think was also passed on to me. A kid in the 50s with emotional problems, was something that was not well understood, and therefore not well treated. So what did we do, we suffered!

I had fun too as a kid, but with a blind eye as to what life really was all about. I guess I hid from it most of my life. The 60s was a bad time for me. I quit school, got involved with drugs and the wrong people. When I should

Green Zone Living

have been getting an education and preparing for adult life, I was having fun with hot cars and poor jobs. Every now and then I would have anxiety, but not know what it was. It cost me jobs, girlfriends, and life in general. All of the 70s and 80s were like that.

It all came to a head when I had my first daughter in 1990. It was like a pressure cooker in my life, building up pressure all my life and finally blowing its top. It was the birth of my daughter, and the birth of reality! This was the start of my panic attacks a few years later, I met Dr. Sohail and that was the second wake up call. As many before, my relationship with my girlfriend was on the rocks, and going down hill fast. She had her own problems, which didn't help the relationship at all. We had a second daughter, but things did not improve between us. I thought this was normal, people not getting along. I had no concept of boundaries because I had never been taught. At first, with Sohail, I didn't take it seriously, it took a long time before I started to listen and learn. And so, the work began. I went from laughing to crying. It took many years of hard work in private sessions and group therapy. What an amazing journey! The light in my life slowly went from RED to AMBER, and finally to GREEN, all the while, fighting with anxiety and panic attacks. But as time went on, the attacks got fewer. There were always a few people in my life that knew what buttons to push to get me in the Red Zone. I slowly filtered them out of my life, including the mother of my children and a friend of 30 years.

I am free of that haunting Red Zone, and although the Amber does appear once in a while, I am quickly under full control and back to the Green. I live better now in almost every way. My approach to boundaries is very good now, however, I do cross the odd one, but just the

Green Zone Living

harmless ones, and just for fun. Now I work, sleep, and live in my Green Zone. My decision-making has become much easer for me. Where I used to stand and argue, I now walk away. Life has been hard for me, but the good part is that I now have two wonderful daughters, a home and most of all, THE GREEN ZONE to control it all. Thanks to Dr. Sohail and Anne without whom I could not have done what I have. Thanks for sticking with me. I still have work to do, it's like when I finish building a car - I now have to polish it.

Dr. K. Sohail & Bette Davis

Susan's Green Zone Story

Green Zone Living Insights

Dear Sohail:

As you know, I was experiencing some problems with my daughter Nadine, with regards to temper tantrums, arguments, and talking down to me, which brought not only her, but me into the Red Zone. It was getting out of control around last March, at which point I discussed how it was affecting my mental state. You and I had discussed introducing the Green, Yellow and Red concept into Nadine's life.

Nadine is not the type of child who would go to her room when told, for a time out. It would become a physical struggle, which was not good for either of us. You had suggested that I walk away and let her sit on her own until she was ready to come and be a part of the family routine again.

Green Zone Living

It was hard for me, but, the first thing I had to learn was to walk out of the room when Nadine would start pushing the buttons that would ultimately lead into a temper tantrum or screaming match. I eventually mastered the art of leaving the room without saying a word. I would stay away for a while and eventually Nadine would come to me. If I did re-enter the area, or Nadine came to me and started pushing again, I would simply walk away again. Nadine eventually realized that I was not going to let her drag me into her Red Zone.

Shortly after learning this skill, I sat down with Nadine and explained the philosophy of the Red, Yellow and Green Zones. We decided to color a circle on the calendar at the end of each day. We followed the following criteria:

Green Day   This would be a happy day with no tantrums, talking back or talking down to me.

Yellow Day   This would be a day where things started to slide down hill but would turn around before flaring into a tantrum or sending me into the Red Zone.

Red Day   This would be a full blown temper tantrum or an argument.

At the end of each day, Nadine would go and color a circle on the calendar to reflect the type of day it had been. The calendar was displayed on the fridge, so it was a reminder each day of our progress during that month.

In the first month, we had more red circles than green and yellow together. After the first month, Nadine and I sat down to discuss the findings. I think she was surprised with herself. I

Green Zone Living

feel that it helped her understand how disruptive her behavior was becoming to our family.

This was when we made an agreement to try and lessen the amount of red circles on the calendar. In order to reach that goal, we chose a treat that was mutually agreed upon as well as a goal that would help reduce the number of yellow or red circles for that month. Of course, the goal was to lessen the number of red and yellow circles each month. If Nadine reached the monthly goal, she would get the treat.

In order to help Nadine, I agreed to inform/warn her when I saw Yellow Zones starting. Eventually, with the warnings, Nadine learned to stop the behavior and cool down before allowing herself to go into a full blown Red Zone.

As the months went on we had less and less red circles on the calendar until eventually we had none. I am happy to say that we got into

Dr. K. Sohail & Bette Davis

a period that there were only green circles on that calendar. After about 3 months, we had a much more peaceful family life and were able to deal with issues much easier.

Nadine and I also had to learn when to talk about upsetting events or frustrations. We have to be able to sit down and talk face to face. We have learned that we have to make sure the other person is ready to listen, has the time to listen and is also able to give full concentration to the subject. All too often in the past, Nadine would be trying to talk to me about a problem when I was either cooking dinner, busy with Steve, putting Adam to bed or I had 4 or 5 kids running around. She would become irate when she thought I didn't understand or wasn't listening. She had to learn to wait until I could give her my full attention.

I found this method worked quickly for us however, I also feel that Nadine's age had

Green Zone Living

something to do with it. I think the older they are the more conscious they are of that calendar. I do feel that using this method with a younger child would take a lot longer but would likely be as effective.

Now in saying all of this, I have to inform you that I have had to reintroduce the method again. I am optimistic that this will work even quicker this time. I have also caught myself not walking out of the room as well as conversations not taking place at appropriate times. This just proves that it is a concept that you have to practice over and over again.

Thank you for helping me to introduce the concept of the Green, Yellow and Red Zones into my children's lives.

Susan

Dr. K. Sohail & Bette Davis

Chapter Five

GREEN ZONE QUESTIONNAIRES

Dear Reader, the following questionnaires are part of the Green Zone Book Series and will assist you in identifying which Emotional Zones the different areas of you life are in, either the Green, Yellow or Red. They are designed to not only give you a point from which to start to build your happy, healthy and peaceful Green Zone Lifestyle but will provide you with feedback as you progress along your journey toward your Green Zone .

If you would rather work with a hard copy, all of our Green Zone Worksheets are

Green Zone Living

available to print on our website at www.greenzoneliving.ca.

NAME _____

DATE _____

SELF-ASSESSMENT QUESTIONNAIRE FOR INDIVIDUALS

Over the years we have developed a questionnaire that is interesting and revealing, yet quite simple to complete. It will introduce you to our concept of the Green, Yellow and Red Zones and help you to discover for yourself the strength and weaknesses of your personality and lifestyle. It will also help you to decide whether you need professional assistance to improve your quality of life.

THE GREEN ZONE

When people choose to live in the Green Zone they are, amongst many other things, pleasant and cheerful. They easily carry on a rational discussion with those around them and, should a difference of opinion arise, they are able to enthusiastically connect with a healthy and constructive inner strength that will encourage the dialogue that helps to resolve or dissolve their conflicts – and most importantly - build bridges that span all differences.

THE YELLOW ZONE

When in the Yellow Zone people feel somewhat distressed. Anxiety, sadness and anger too often rule their thoughts and actions. Because of their discomfort, they are unable to communicate with others effectively and are poorly equipped to deal with stressful situations or interpersonal conflicts. This Zone is a slippery slope that often leads to many problems that await them when they cannot hold on and fall into the Red Zone.

Dr. K. Sohail & Bette Davis

THE RED ZONE

Those who occupy the Red Zone are extremely unhappy, emotionally exhausted, usually maintain a high state of hidden anger and are extremely distressed. They often lose control and become abusive or completely withdrawn from others, sometimes fleeing to escape — even from themselves! They have great difficulty dealing with stressful situations, unable to have a rational discussion to resolve or dissolve their interpersonal conflicts. At times they lack the will to take care of their personal appearance, overlook proper nourishment and avoid being responsible for family members in their charge.

QUESTIONNAIRE

1. What Zone colors have you lived in most of your life? (If more than one, use a percentage figure to show the comparison.)

Green Zone Living

	Green	Yellow	Red
Birth to 15 years			
16 years to 30 years			
31 years to present			

2. In what Zones do you presently spend your time?

	Green	Yellow	Red
Mostly			
Occasionally			
Rarely			

3. What Zones do you presently live in within your family environment?

	Green	Yellow	Red
Mostly			
Occasionally			
Rarely			

4. In your work environment, what Zones do you presently live in?

	Green	Yellow	Red
Mostly			
Occasionally			
Rarely			

Green Zone Living

5. In your present social environment, what Zones do you live in?

	Green	Yellow	Red
Mostly			
Occasionally			
Rarely			

6. If needed, what three things can you do to recover from the Yellow and Red Zones?

A.	
B.	
C.	

7. What are the three most important things you can do to restrain yourself from falling into the Yellow and Red Zones?

A.	
B.	
C	

8. List your significant relationships and then decide in what Zone each lives.

Name	Relationship	Green	Yellow	Red
1.				
2.				
3.				
4.				
5.				
6.				
7.				
8.				
9.				
10.				

9. With which significant relationships can you comfortably discuss the concept of Green, Yellow, and Red Zones that will improve the quality of that relationship? (Please refer to item 8 above and circle the appropriate numbers.)

10. In which significant relationships can you discuss the issue of finding a Mediator or a

Green Zone Living

Therapist? (Please refer to item 8 above and add a square box around the appropriate numbers.)

11. Which significant relationships can you dissolve (have little or no communication with in future) because there is no hope or willingness to resolve conflicts that could improve the quality of the relationship? (Please refer to item 8 above and draw an X through the appropriate numbers.)

12. List social, professional, political, religious or cultural organizations you belong to and then decide the Zone you live in with each one.

Name	Green	Yellow	Red
1.			
2.			
3.			
4.			
5.			
6.			
7.			
8.			

9.			
10.			

13. What five things can you do to live regularly in the Green Zone?

A.	
B.	
C.	
D.	
E.	

14. Do you need professional help to live in the Green Zone? Explain why.

COMMENT

When you live in the Green Zone during most aspects of your life, you are very likely leading a happy, healthy and balanced life. When the Yellow Zone causes pain during much of your life, you need to think seriously about how to

Green Zone Living

improve the quality of your life by immediately discussing it with significant people you trust. When the Red Zone dominates your life, you need to act immediately to seek professional counseling to bring fulfillment and joy into your life.

Dr. K. Sohail & Bette Davis

DISCOVERING YOUR GREEN DAY

As you choose to spend more and more time in your Green Zone, you can track your progress by using the chart that follows. Make photocopies so that you can have a record of how you were able to fine-tune your awareness and your responses over time.

DISCOVERING YOUR GREEN DAY

NAME_____ DAY_____ DATE_____		
ZONE	HOURS SPENT	WHAT WAS HAPPENING?
GREEN		
YELLOW		
RED		

© Green Zone Living

NAME _____

DATE _____

SELF-ASSESSMENT QUESTIONNAIRE FOR COUPLES

To have a better understanding of the quality and dynamics of intimate relationships we have devised the following questionnaire. Completing this questionnaire will help you and your partner to assess whether you are loving in the Green, Yellow or Red Zones.

This questionnaire not only provides insights into the perceptions of partners but also highlights the differences. The answers are quite helpful in opening up a dialogue between spouses and also with your therapist.

Green Zone Living

Please enter a number indicating your response to each question.

Red……..1….Not at all

Yellow….3….Moderately

Green…..5….Very much

ISSUES	QUESTIONS	SCORE
TRUST	1. Do you trust your spouse? 2. Does your spouse trust you?	……….. ………
CONTROL	3. Do you feel free to be your natural self in your partner's company? 4. Do you feel your partner feels free to be his/her natural self in your company?	……… ………
BOUNDARIES	5. Do you respect your partner's relationship with his / her friends and family? 6. Does your partner respect your relationship with your friends and family?	……… ………

Dr. K. Sohail & Bette Davis

INTIMACY	7. Do you express your affection and love freely and spontaneously?	....
	8. Does your partner express his / her affection and love freely and spontaneously?	....
VALUES/ LIFESTYLES	9. Do you respect your partner's lifestyle and values?	....
	10. Does your partner respect your lifestyle and values?	....
CONFLICTS	11. Are you able to resolve/ dissolve conflicts?	....
	12. Is your partner able to resolve/ dissolve conflicts?	....
SUPPORT	13. Do your friends support your relationship?	....
	14. Do your partner's friends support your relationship?	....
	15. Does your family support your relationship?	....
	16. Does your partner's family support your relationship?	....
	17. Does your community support your relationship?	....

Green Zone Living

	18. Does your partner's community support your relationship?	....
FUTURE	19. Do you see a bright future for your relationship?	....
	20. Does your partner see a bright future for your relationship?	....
	TOTAL SCORE	....

© Green Zone Living

NOTE. If you would like to elaborate upon any of your answers, please do so on a separate sheet.

RESULTS

If you are loving in the Green Zone (Score 80-100), most likely you are enjoying a happy and healthy intimate relationship.

Dr. K. Sohail & Bette Davis

If you are loving in the Yellow Zone (Score 60-80), you can try for a few months to help yourself to get to your Green Zone, and if you are unsuccessful, you should seek professional help.

If you are loving in the Red Zone (Score 1-60), you need to seriously consider getting professional help.

Green Zone Living

WORKING IN GREEN ZONE
QUESTIONNAIRE

We have devised the following questionnaire to assist you in determining whether you are working in your Green, Yellow or Red Zone. Completing it will be the first step in allowing you to be more aware of your Emotional Zones at work. Your answers will highlight for you where you can begin to address your concerns.

To complete it, first circle the answers that apply to you, and then count the number of answers in the GREEN column.

#	QUESTION	GREEN	YELLOW	RED
1.	Do you enjoy the type of work you do?	YES	SOMEWHAT	NO
2.	Do you feel stimulated/ challenged at work?	YES	SOMEWHAT	NO

Dr. K. Sohail & Bette Davis

3.	Does your job allow you to express your best qualities?	YES	SOMEWHAT	NO
4.	Do you enjoy walking / driving to work?	YES	SOMEWHAT	NO
5.	Do you like the physical environment you work in?	YES	SOMEWHAT	NO
6.	Do you like working with your co-workers?	YES	SOMEWHAT	NO
7.	Do you like working with your manager /administration?	YES	SOMEWHAT	NO
8.	Do you feel respected at work?	YES	SOMEWHAT	NO
9.	Do you feel appreciated at work?	YES	SOMEWHAT	NO
10.	Is your workload manageable?	YES	SOMEWHAT	NO

Green Zone Living

11.	Do you take work home?	NO	SOMETIMES	YES
12.	Do you feel that you are working harder and getting less done?	NO	SOMEWHAT	YES
13.	Do you feel tired at the end of the workday / week?	NO	SOMEWHAT	YES
14.	Do you take breaks during the day / week to re-energize yourself?	YES	SOMETIMES	NO
15.	Does it take most of your time off to recuperate from work demands?	NO	SOMETIMES	YES
16.	Do you take vacation time each year?	YES	SOMETIMES	NO
17.	Do you feel you have lost some of your concern/ caring for your customers?	NO	SOMEWHAT	YES

Dr. K. Sohail & Bette Davis

18.	Do you have physical symptoms (headache, backache, chest pain) related to stress at work?	NO	SOMETIMES	YES
19.	Are you irritable with your co-workers, family or friends because of work tension?	NO	SOMETIMES	YES
20.	Do your work and family lives conflict with each other?	NO	SOMEWHAT	YES
21.	Can you express your concerns at work?	YES	SOMETIMES	NO
22.	Can you resolve conflicts at work?	YES	SOMETIMES	NO
23.	Are your interactions with your co-workers respectful?	YES	SOMEWHAT	NO

Green Zone Living

24.	Can you take sick leave, annual leave, etc. without feeling guilty?	YES	SOMETIMES	NO
25.	If needed would you be able to get extended leave, like disability?	YES	SOMETIMES	NO
26.	Do you have the independence and authority needed to do your work?	YES	SOMEWHAT	NO
27.	Are you uncertain because of threatened layoffs or changes in your workplace?	NO	SOMEWHAT	YES
28.	If you had a choice would you take another job?	NO	SOMETIMES	YES

Dr. K. Sohail & Bette Davis

29.	Would you be willing to get professional help to cope with stress at work?	YES	SOMEWHAT	NO
30.	What Zone do you mostly live in outside work?	GREEN	YELLOW	RED
	TOTAL # of responses in the GREEN column.			

© Green Zone Living

RESULTS

• If you are working in your Green Zone **(Score 24 - 30),** most likely you are enjoying your work and have developed healthy relationships in the workplace.

• If you are working in your Yellow Zone **(Score 18 - 24),** it is recommended that you use the techniques that we have outlined in this book to get yourself into your Green Zone. If after a

Green Zone Living

few months you have not been successful then you should seek professional help.

• If you are working in your Red Zone **(Score 1 - 18),** you need to seriously consider seeking professional help.

The Happy, Healthy and Peaceful
GREENZONE Living 7 Step Program

STEP ONE – Becoming aware of your
Emotional Zones, either Green, Yellow, or Red.

STEP TWO - Recognizing changes in your
Emotional Zones.

•   Identify three things that push you to
the Yellow and Red Zones.

STEP THREE - Recovering from the Yellow and
Red Zones.

•   Identify three things you can do to get
back to your Green Zone.

STEP FOUR - Restraining from going into the
Yellow and Red Zones.

Green Zone Living

• Identify three things you can do to stay in your Green Zone.

STEP FIVE -Creating Green Zone Relationships.

• Make a list of all significant relationships and decide what Zone they are in and how you will deal with the Yellow and Red Zones relationships.

STEP SIX - Creating Green Zone Systems.

• Identify the Zones of your Family, Work and Social Systems.

STEP SEVEN - Creating Your Green Zone Lifestyle

• Discover your Special Gift - Creating, Sharing and Serving.

Dr. K. Sohail & Bette Davis

CREATING GREEN ZONE PHILOSOPHY

When I reflect on my past, I realize that quite early in my life I had developed a compassion for the suffering humanity. Witnessing so many men, women and children struggling and hurting all around me, motivated me to find ways to decrease their pain and suffering. I had a dream of helping human beings become healthy, happy and peaceful. I wanted to join hands with all those who wanted to create a peaceful world together. Now I realize that my compassion for suffering humanity and my dream of a peaceful world, inspired me to become a writer, a doctor, a psychotherapist and a humanist and create Green Zone Philosophy. My Green Zone Philosophy is my gift to the suffering humanity.

Sohail
February 5th, 2013

Green Zone Living

Publications from the Green Zone Library

<u>**Books**</u>

From Islam to Secular Humanism

The Myth of the Chosen One

Love, Sex and Marriage

\-   Dr. K. Sohail and Bette Davis RN BN MN

The Art of Living in Your Green Zone

The Art of Loving in Your Green Zone

The Art of Working in Your Green Zone

\-   Dr. K. Sohail and Bette Davis RN BN MN

Prophets of Violence, Prophets of Peace

<u>**Video Documentaries**</u>

Domestic Violence

  Breaking the Cycle

Marital Problems

  Growing Alone — Growing Together

Mixed Marriages

  Intimate Encounters

Dr. K. Sohail & Bette Davis

Psychotherapy

> *Encounters with Depression*
> *Green Zone Stories*
> *Green Zone Lifestyle*

Green Zone Publishing

213 Byron Street South

Whitby Ontario Canada L1N4P7

Please contact us through our website at www.greenzoneliving.ca

Green Zone Living

About Green Zone Living and its Authors

In the contemporary world, day-to-day life for most people has become so stressful that: one in four women and one in ten men suffer from depression, one marriage in three ends in divorce and the number of people going on sick leave and getting burnt out from toxic work environments is increasing rapidly.

In such turbulent and traumatic social circumstances, a number of mental health professionals and philosophers worldwide have accepted the challenge to find creative ways to deal with life's dilemmas and dreams. Two such professionals are psychotherapists Dr. K. Sohail and Bette Davis. Based on their more than fifty years of psychotherapy experience with hundreds of individuals, couples and families, they have developed the concept of Green Zone

Dr. K. Sohail & Bette Davis

Living. Green Zone Living is based on the Green Zone Philosophy that inspires people to create a healthy, happy and peaceful Green Zone Lifestyle. The Green Zone Philosophy has already helped a large number of people not only to deal with their emotional and relationship problems but also improve the quality of their lives.

Green Zone Living